coffee & bites

Susie Theodorou

photography by Clive Streeter

MURDOCH
BOOKS

contents

6 introduction

8 perfect coffee

24 with morning coffee

46 in the afternoon

70 after dinner

94 index

96 coffee directory

introduction

For many of us, the day is punctuated by coffee and

its attendant pleasures, from the morning's first

mellow café au lait and croissant to the rich, dark

espresso enjoyed with truffles after dinner.

The tantalizing aroma and complex flavour of this

stimulating brew cries out for a little something to

nibble alongside. Something crisp, something flaky,

something buttery, something chocolatey. Just a bite.

perfect coffee

what's in a bean?

From tiny beginnings in Abyssinia in the sixth century AD, coffee has become a multi-billion dollar industry, and is now grown throughout the world's tropical zones. The beans, green at first, are found in pairs at the centre of 'cherries', which ripen to a dark red and hang in clusters from trees. With the outer skin and flesh removed, many coffees will improve if kept for up to 10 years. Before the beans are ready for use they are roasted, and it is this process that gives us the warm, inviting aroma that greets us when we walk into our favourite coffee shop.

the bean groups

Of the more than 50 species of coffee plant, just two – arabica, indigenous to Ethiopia and robusta, first discovered in the Congo – make up the vast majority of the world's production.

Arabica

This is the most sought-after species and accounts for 70 per cent of the world's output. It is grown at approximately 1,000 – 2,000 metres above sea level, but the higher the altitude, the better the quality. Those grown at upwards of 1,500 metres can be given labels such as Supreme, AA or Estate. By a freak force of nature, good-quality arabica beans contain about half the caffeine level of low-quality robusta beans. Arabica beans are fairly flat and green in colour with silver blue shades. This species is cultivated in Ethiopia, Jamaica, Brazil, Colombia and Central America.

Robusta

A hardy bean that grows at lower altitudes, and more often than not, at sea level, the robusta needs very little rainfall. This bean makes up 25 per cent of the world's coffee production and, though inferior to the arabica, is still an important part of the coffee industry, used predominantly in blends of ground or instant coffee. It is also very well suited to the espresso method of making coffee. The robusta is found in the highest quality espresso blends, as it helps in the development of the 'crema' on the top of espresso coffee. The bean is fairly small, tends to be oval in shape, and before roasting, varies in colour from shades of yellow to light brown. Robusta beans are cultivated in parts of Brazil, West and Central Africa, and throughout South East Asia.

what to look for in a coffee bean

Acidity

A pleasant sharpness on the tip of the tongue, similar to that given by dry white wine. Acidity can be fruity, as in Kenyan coffee, or of a metallic quality, as in coffees from Mexico. Without acidity, coffee tastes flat.

Body

This describes the feeling of the coffee in your mouth – the heaviness, thickness and richness felt on the tongue. Kenyan and Ethiopian coffees tend to be full bodied, those from South East Asia are medium bodied and South and Central American coffees are light bodied. Coffee with a heavier body will maintain more of its flavour when milk is added to it.

Aroma

This is the scent of the oils that are released when beans are roasted. High-quality coffees will contain two to three times the quantity of such oils as inferior ones. South American beans can be recognized by their extra-shiny appearance after roasting.

Flavour

Professional coffee tasters use various terms to describe the flavour of coffee. Desirable ones include 'earthy', 'gamey' and 'fruity'. 'Earthy' is a heavy sweetness, 'gamey' a milky, yoghurty quality, and 'fruity' a pleasant, citrus taste. The term 'rubbery' speaks for itself, but other less favourable descriptions include 'green' and 'Rioy'. 'Green' describes a harsh, grassy flavour that develops in incorrectly roasted beans, and 'Rioy' is a medicinal taste that comes about as a result of poor harvesting. When a coffee is described as 'well-balanced', it means that the acidity, the body and the flavour are all in harmonious agreement.

coffee beans

Even though there are just two main species of beans, coffee is a substance of infinite variety. Altitude, climate, soil type and harvesting methods all have a part to play in determining how it will taste. On the whole, you will find that shops sell only arabica beans as single varieties – robustas are used mainly in blends. Just sniffing a handful of beans won't help you work out how the coffee will taste, though, so before you start experimenting, it pays to bear in mind the qualities you can expect from some of the varieties most commonly sold.

types of arabica beans

Brazilian Bourbon Santos
Only the first few harvests of this crop, which yields a medium-bodied, low-acidity coffee, can be described as Bourbon. After this, it will be called Santos, which has low acidity, medium body and mellow flavour. *Bourbon Santos should be medium roast, Santos medium or dark roast.*

Colombian San Augustin
Grown in the Huila district of south west Colombia, this has well-balanced acidity, medium body, and is stronger than Brazilian varieties. *Medium roast.*

Mexican Maragogype
This is a variety known for its size – it's often referred to as the elephant bean. It has delicate acidity and medium body. *Medium or dark roast.*

Costa Rican San Jose
A good coffee bean with a delicate flavour and fine, subtle acidity. This coffee is perfect for filter and cafetière coffee makers. *Medium or dark roast.*

Jamaican Blue Mountain
In its purest form, this is the finest coffee grown in Jamaica. It has perfect balance of flavour and acidity and a delicate flavour with a pleasant lingering aftertaste. *Medium roast.*

Yemeni Mocha
This bean has spicy undertones with a wine-like acidity. It has a distinctive cocoa flavour, and is essential for making the best Turkish coffee. *Medium roast.*

Kenyan AA or Estate
This bean is Kenya's number one. It has tremendous body, a rich, fruity acidity and a faintly blackcurranty flavour, with a beautifully rich aroma that is almost sweet. *Medium or dark roast.*

Kenyan Peaberry
A superior bean. Whereas in most coffee cherries there are two beans, in this variety there is just one round one, which contains all of the concentrated flavour of two. The Peaberry roasts evenly and has a sharpness that gives it a good, full body. *Medium or dark roast.*

Ethiopian Mocha
Arabica coffee is indigenous to Ethiopia, and some of the coffee produced here is still gathered from wild trees. This bean has a hint of cocoa and is full bodied and gamey, with less acidity than some full-bodied beans. *Medium roast.*

Harar Longberry
This is another Ethiopian bean with a wine-like, gamey taste. It is heavier and richer than the Mocha, with a pungent aroma. *Medium roast.*

Tanzanian Kilimanjaro
This has a rich flavour and delicate acidity, though it is not as sharp as the Kenyan AA. *Medium or dark roast.*

Monsooned Malabar Mysore
This Indian bean has a pleasantly mellow, full flavour with gentle acidity. The 'monsooning' refers to a process during which unwashed beans are exposed to dampness and then to hot monsoon winds to give a characteristic mellow taste. *Medium roast.*

Java
A medium-bodied Indonesian bean. It has a smooth, mellow flavour with spicy overtones. *Medium roast.*

Sumatra Blue
Another Indonesian arabica, this is very heavy bodied, rich and smooth, and can be an acquired taste. *Medium roast.*

roasting

When picked and dried, the coffee bean is green in colour and has no scent. As it is roasted, the sugars within the bean caramelize, creating coffee oil, which is responsible for the flavour and aroma of the bean. Each variety requires a different level of roast, in order to bring out the particular characteristics of that bean and depending on how the resultant coffee is to be used.

good colour

A good coffee roaster must be part artist, part scientist in order to maintain quality and consistency. As they roast, beans expand and turn anything from light caramel to dark chocolate in colour (they should never become so dark as to appear black). If insufficiently roasted, the bean will produce a colourless infusion, with a rough and astringent taste. If over-roasted, the coffee will be black, bitter and unpleasant. Beans are either roasted in a rotating drum heated by gas or wood (the drum method) or by being tumbled over a current of hot air (the air method). In both cases, the beans must be cooled very quickly to stop the roasting from continuing – this is done by spreading the beans out and applying cold air to them.

levels of roasting

Light roast

Lightly roasted beans are pale in colour and produce coffee with a sharp, acidic taste. This roast can be used for all types of coffee making, with the exception of espresso.

Medium roast

Slightly darker in colour and with a satin-like lustre, the flavour is fuller than a lightly roasted bean, with a somewhat bittersweet tang. It is a mild or medium-strong coffee, depending on the variety of bean that is used. All coffee brewing methods can be used, although espresso is not recommended.

Dark roast

This should be darker than medium roast, but not black. The characteristic smoky flavour is ideally suited to coffees that are to be served strong, whether for breakfast or after dinner. This level of roasting is good for espresso, too.

Very dark roast

Also known as Continental roast, this is a very powerful coffee – perfect served with or after very rich food, especially desserts. All coffee-making methods can be used, but this type of roast should be served black or with very little milk.

Home roasting

To roast at home, you need to be a really committed coffee lover – this process can smell the house out! Spread the beans in a single layer over the bottom of a heavy-based frying pan. Stir them constantly over a fierce heat and watch the changing colour of the beans to achieve your chosen roast. The easiest way to tell if the beans are sufficiently roasted is to bite into one – you need to be sure that they're roasted right the way through. Roasting is a hit and miss process, requiring a certain amount of experimentation in order to achieve consistent results.

When to blend?

Some coffee blenders believe that roasting each variety of bean separately prior to blending gives optimum flavour, whereas others say that blending before roasting lets the flavour of the mixed beans integrate more fully. The solution to the dilemma remains very much a matter of personal taste.

decaffeination

The level of caffeine in a cup of coffee can vary slightly according to the type of bean used and the level of roast (with darker roasts containing slightly less caffeine). The most important variable is the brewing method used. Because of concerns over caffeine's effects on the body, decaffeinated coffee has become popular. Decaffeination usually happens before the beans are roasted and any type of bean can be used. The beans are soaked thoroughly in water and then the caffeine is removed using carbon, solvents or carbon dioxide.

grinding

Although most specialist shops are better equipped for grinding coffee than most kitchens, for the enthusiast and flavour perfectionist, coffee beans should be ground at home just before brewing. How finely depends on the method of coffee making to be used. Generally speaking (and with the exception of Turkish coffee), the less time the water and the coffee are in contact, the finer the grind should be.

grinders

There are two types of grinders you can use at home, both of which can create grinds of varying coarseness. Blade grinders (above) are the most common. These repeatedly slice the beans, so the fineness of the grind is decided by how long the machine runs. However, the grind can be inconsistent. Burr grinders (left and above, centre) can be electric or manual. These crush the beans to a pre-set coarseness and give a much more even grind than blade grinders. For a pulverized grind, use a pestle and mortar.

which grind?

Pulverized coffee This is a very fine flour-like powder used for making Turkish coffee in an ibrik (see page 19).
Very fine grind This is the best grind for filter coffee.
Fine grind Espresso machines or pots need a fine grind of coffee with a little texture.
Medium grind This should be used for cafetières or percolators.
Medium-coarse grind It is best to use this for making coffee using the jug method.

storing coffee

It is important to keep coffee sealed and chilled once ground. This slows the rate of oxidation, which makes coffee stale, and also prevents it picking up surrounding aromas and flavours. In the freezer, whole beans stored in special valve bags will last 6 months, 3 months if ground. In airtight containers, whole beans will last 3 months and ground coffee 2 months. Whole beans in sealed containers can be stored in the fridge for 2–3 months and for 1–2 months if ground.

jug method

filter method

stove-top filter pot

cafetière method

filter method

espresso machine

brewing methods

The way you choose to brew your coffee depends on many things. The time of day, how much time you have, how strong you want it to be, how many people you are serving and – not least – the equipment that you have to hand. Many people, too, have a particular favourite simply because they enjoy the ritual of preparing coffee that way. The fun lies in experimenting to find a method to suit you.

jug method

This is the most basic method of making coffee, and probably the one cowboys in the USA would have used over their campfires! Coffee and cold water are simply placed together in a coffee pot (about 1 tablespoon coffee per 200ml [6½fl oz] water) and brought gently to the boil, at which point the coffee is ready to strain into cups to serve.

cafetière method

In this method, water is poured directly onto coffee grounds, and then separated with a plunger. To achieve the ultimate cup of cafetière coffee, warm the pot first and, for a 4-cup or 0.75 litre (24fl oz) model, spoon in 4 heaped tablespoons freshly ground coffee. Half fill the jug with boiling hot water, give the grains a stir, then pour in the remaining water in a long, steady stream – filling the cafetière right to the top. Put on the lid and place the plunger on the surface of the water. Leave for a minute for the beans to infuse, then push down the plunger and pour.

filter method

Ground coffee is placed in a filter and hot water is poured on, or dripped on if a machine is used, producing a clear cup of coffee, free from any suspended grounds. For each person, use approximately 2 tablespoons per 200ml (6½fl oz) water. As convenient as electric filter machines are, they will cause the coffee to become bitter if it is left to stand on the hot plate for too long – any longer than about 20 minutes and the coffee will have lost its flavour. Another way of keeping filter coffee warm – popular in Scandinavian countries – is to pour the coffee directly into a warmed vacuum flask, or, indeed, filter the coffee directly into the flask.

ibrik

This is a pear-shaped metal pot that can be placed on the stove and is used for making Turkish coffee. Use 1 heaped teaspoon pulverized ground coffee to 90ml (3¼fl oz) water per person. Stir in a little sugar, if desired, then allow the coffee to come to the boil slowly (this is imperative if the coffee is to have the essential foamy head). Remove from the heat, stir and leave to rest for a few seconds. Pour into small cups for a very strong black coffee, which will leave a sludgy residue at the bottom of the cup.

percolator

Here the coffee is placed in a filter within the pot, which has a tube that runs up through the centre and down into the water in the base. The percolator is placed on the stove and when the water boils, it rises up the tube and is then sprinkled over the ground coffee. The water soaks into the coffee, and then drips back into the water in order to rise back up the tube. As soon as the water boils, take it off the heat – the water will continue to rise up the tube. If the coffee is left to boil, it will become bitter. Electric percolators are also available, and these switch off automatically once the water has boiled. Use 6 tablespoons coffee per 4-cup 0.75 litres (24fl oz) water.

espresso making

You can make espresso at home using a stove-top pot. These come in two parts that screw together, with a metal filter in the middle in which about one tablespoon finely ground coffee per person is placed and tamped down. The water (about 75ml [2½fl oz] per person) is put in the lower part of the pot, which is placed over a medium heat. As it boils, water and steam bubble through the coffee to emerge in the top part of the pot for pouring. Or, you can invest in a machine that will do the same thing, either at the push of a button or the pump of a handle. See page 96 for recommendations.

espresso shots

You can create any cup of coffee at home – you don't have to stick to the cafetière, nor do you need to invest in a big, fancy machine. The basic espresso actually forms the basis of many other coffee bar requests, so cappuccinos, lattes or cold caffe freddos can all be included in your repertoire. The techniques for making a delicious cup of your chosen coffee are simple, so get brewing!

espresso

A single shot of concentrated dark-coloured coffee, topped with a light brown foamy crema, formed by the pressure with which the water is forced through the coffee. The crema should be resilient enough to hold a spoonful of sugar for a couple of seconds.

caffe latte freddo

Hot espresso is mixed with cold milk – the proportions are one-third espresso to two-thirds milk – and shaken with ice. Ideally, the coffee should be strained into a large glass, but you can serve it with the ice, if you prefer. Serve with a couple of long straws.

espresso variations

Americano – an espresso diluted with hot water, also known as a caffe grande or a long espresso. *Ristretto* – an extra-strong espresso. *Romano* – espresso served with a twist of lemon peel. *Corretto* – espresso 'corrected' with a dash of amaretto, sambuca or grappa.

caffe freddo

A shot of espresso
(sweetened if desired, while
hot), which is cooled down
by shaking with ice in a
cocktail shaker. The coffee is
then quickly strained into a
chilled glass – the coffee will
have a fine layer of crema.
Caffe freddo is served at the
end of an evening meal.

coffee granita

This is a grainy iced coffee.
Mix 300ml (10fl oz) freshly
made espresso with 200g
(7oz/1 cup) soft brown sugar
and 50ml (1¾fl oz) brandy,
then freeze, stirring every
two hours until a light crystal
texture is formed. Serve with
a spoon as a delicious, cool
end to a meal.

espresso macchiato

A shot of espresso, served in
a small glass or cup stained
(which is what macchiato
means) with a dab of hot
milk froth. Despite being
officially a milky coffee, one
can just about get away with
drinking this after dinner,
even in Italy where such
things are frowned upon!

froth it up

Once upon a time (actually only a few years ago), you needed a coffee machine with a steaming device to froth the milk for cappuccino or latte – and even then, the pressure was never quite strong enough! Perversely, in the hi-tech 21st century, we have found an easier way: a cafetière can froth up milk brilliantly. Skimmed milk works best. Warm it in a pan to just below boiling point and transfer it to a cafetière so that the milk comes one-third of the way up – you must leave room for the milk to expand. Pump the plunger about ten times to create your froth. Leftover milk cannot be reheated and refrothed. Small battery-operated hand milk frothers can also be used – these really are good! – but for the ultimate low-tech solution, pour the heated milk into a plastic mineral water bottle, close tightly and shake away!

hot milk anyone?

When milk is added to an espresso, the coffee takes on a whole new meaning – a new drink is created and the flavour of the coffee is given a different tone. The addition of milk can even affect the time of day that the coffee is consumed. Most milky coffees are considered to be breakfast fare, to the extent that drinking cappuccino after midday in Italy is a real no-no!

cappuccino

This is about one-third espresso, one-third hot milk topped with one-third froth. This should not be extremely milky and the flavour of the coffee should come through. A true aficionado would never sprinkle the foam with chocolate, as is sometimes seen in coffee shops.

caffe latte

One part espresso to four parts milk – milkier-tasting than the cappuccino. The milk and coffee should be poured simultaneously into a thick glass. This drink has largely been popularized by the many American-style coffee shops that have appeared in recent years.

café au lait

This is a popular breakfast drink in France as well as in Spain, where it's known as cafe con leche. Made by topping a shot of espresso with hot milk, it is usually served in a bowl. This type of coffee is every European child's introduction to the wonderful world of coffee.

with morning coffee

croque monsieur

The gruyère cheese paste is the component that gives this croque monsieur its authenticity. Recipes vary from one French café to the next, but whichever one you favour, this sandwich is a classic café bar snack to enjoy with a caffe grande (long black coffee).

15g (½oz) butter
1 tablespoon plain
   (all-purpose) flour
100ml (3½fl oz/½ cup) milk
150g (5oz/1¼ cups) gruyère
   cheese, coarsely grated
salt and freshly ground
   black pepper
smooth Dijon mustard to taste
4–8 slices thin country bread,
   depending on size
extra butter to spread
75g (3oz) thin slices
   country ham

Coffee choice
caffe grande made with
   dark roasted Tanzanian
   Kilimanjaro beans

Melt the butter in a saucepan until foaming. Mix in the flour and cook for 1 minute. Gradually stir in the milk and cook over a gentle heat until thick; cook for a further minute to cook out the flour taste. Away from the heat, stir in the cheese and season to taste, also adding as much mustard as you like. The sauce must be of a very thick consistency – like a paste. Set aside.

If you are using large slices of bread, you will only need two per person; if small, use four. Spread the bread with butter on one side, then put the bread, buttered-side down, on a clean surface and spread the slices with the cheese paste. Top half the bread with the ham, then sandwich with the other slices of bread, cheese-side down.

Heat a heavy-based frying pan until hot. Add the sandwiches and cook over a low heat for 5–8 minutes until golden on the base, then flip over and continue to cook for a further 5 minutes. Serve immediately.
   Serves 2

tip
When you are in a hurry, there is nothing to stop you cheating a little with a few slices of gruyère cheese in place of the paste.

breakfast muffins

raspberry streusal muffins

breakfast muffins

These muffins are for those who prefer a slightly less sweet cake. They can be made in muffin cases but if you use taller moulds you will find that the mixture rises much better – and they also look better. Use Provençal glazed drinking mugs or look out for small glass pots, especially French-style jam pots – the small ones make excellent ovenproof cooking containers.

175g (6oz/1½ cups) self-raising
  (self-rising) flour
½ teaspoon ground cinnamon
2 teaspoons baking powder
25g (1oz) wheat bran
2 tablespoons soft brown sugar
finely grated rind of 1 lemon
50g (2oz/¼ cup) unsalted butter
75ml (2½fl oz/⅓ cup) clear honey
2 large eggs
250ml (8fl oz/1 cup) buttermilk
1 small carrot, peeled
  and finely grated
50g (2oz/⅓ cup) raisins
1 tablespoon rolled oats

Coffee choice
caffe latte or cappuccino
  made with dark roasted
  Kenyan AA beans

Preheat the oven to 190°C, 170–180°C fan-assisted (375°F, gas mark 5). Use about 8 Provençal glazed drinking mugs or thick glass ovenproof jam pots of varying sizes from 150ml (5fl oz/⅔ cup) capacity to 200ml (6½fl oz/¾ cup). Line the bases with greased greaseproof (waxed) paper.

Sift the flour with the ground cinnamon and baking powder. Then, stir in the wheat bran, sugar and lemon rind. Melt the butter, then beat in the honey and eggs. Pour into the dry mixture together with the buttermilk. Mix well to form a lumpy batter. Fold in the carrot and raisins; the mixture should be quite uneven.

Spoon the batter into the prepared mugs – about two-thirds of the way up. Sprinkle over the rolled oats and bake for 30 minutes until well risen and cracked on the surface. Allow the muffins to cool slightly before turning out. Serve warm or cold.
    Makes 8

raspberry streusal muffins

Sweet fruit muffins have now become traditional breakfast food all over the Western world. The streusal on top of the raspberry muffins gives them a crunchy finish. Making these muffins in glazed straight-sided ovenproof mugs allows the streusal to rise and set well above the paper cases. Use double paper muffin cases inside the mugs as they lend the cooked muffin extra support.

175g (6oz/1½ cups) self-raising
   (self-rising) flour
1 teaspoon baking powder
115g (4oz/½ cup) caster
   (superfine) sugar
200ml (6½fl oz/¾ cup) buttermilk
1 large egg
115g (4oz/½ cup) unsalted
   butter, melted
150g (5oz/1¼ cups)
   fresh raspberries

For the streusal topping
100g (3½oz/1 cup) icing
   (confectioner's) sugar
75g (3oz/¾ cup) self-raising
   (self-rising) flour
85g (3¼oz/⅓ cup) unsalted
   butter, melted

Coffee choice
filter coffee made with
   full-bodied medium roasted
   Ethiopian Mocha beans

Preheat the oven to 180°C, 160–170°C fan-assisted (350°F, gas mark 4). Lightly grease inside the top half of 8 tall, glazed mugs with a little butter. Then, drop 2 paper muffin cases into each mug.

Sift the flour and baking powder into a large bowl. Stir in the sugar. Add the buttermilk, egg and melted butter and beat until combined – the mixture should be a little lumpy. Fold in the raspberries with a large metal spoon.

For the streusal, sift the icing (confectioner's) sugar into a large bowl and stir in the flour. Add the butter and rub into the mixture until large crumbs form.

Spoon the muffin batter into the prepared mugs, completely filling the muffin case and a little extra. Drop the streusal topping on top. Place the mugs in a roasting tin or baking tray and bake for 30–35 minutes until the muffins are well risen, cracked on the top and golden brown. Loosen the sides of the streusal muffins with a thin-bladed knife. Cool slightly before turning out of the mugs. Remove one of the muffin cases from each muffin to reveal a beautiful raspberry marbled effect. Serve warm or cold.

   Makes 8

melting salmon, crème fraîche and caper flat bread

The assortment and accessibility of flat breads are many – you'll find the best variety in Middle Eastern and Mediterranean food shops. Flat breads include the familiar pitta breads of all shapes and sizes, khobez (round pocket breads), the large sheets of village bread, such as the herbed Lebanese, or the extra thick filo pastry from Turkish shops, called yufka.

2 white khobez (or pitta breads),
   about 20cm (8in) diameter
4 tablespoons crème fraîche
8 slices smoked salmon
juice of ½ a lemon
freshly ground black pepper
50g (2oz) watercress
2 tablespoons capers, rinsed
lemon wedges to serve

Coffee choice
caffe grande made with
   full-bodied, dark roasted
   Kenyan Peaberry beans

Preheat a ridged sandwich maker, heavy-based frying pan or griddle.
Open out the pocket breads and spread each with 2 tablespoons crème fraîche.
Continue to fill each with 3–4 slices smoked salmon, a squeeze of lemon juice and plenty of freshly ground black pepper. Add a handful of watercress, then top with 1 tablespoon capers (depending on your taste) and close the bread.

Toast each filled khobez in the sandwich maker for 1 minute, or 1 minute on each side in a frying pan or on a griddle. Cut into quarters and serve with extra lemon juice.
   Serves 2

other flavour combinations

artichoke, rocket and parmesan

Open out 2 sheets round thick Turkish yufka. Fill the inner 15cm (6in) square of each with half of: 4 marinated artichoke hearts, chopped, 6 black olives, chopped, 115g (4oz) parmesan cheese, sliced into shavings, 75g (3oz) rocket (arugula), chopped, salt and freshly ground black pepper. Fold the edges over to form a square. Cook on a preheated griddle for 5 minutes on the folded side and 3–5 minutes on the other. Halve to serve.

spinach and fontina cheese

Melt 25g (1oz) butter in a pan and sauté 1 small onion, finely chopped, until soft. Add 350g (12oz) baby spinach leaves and cook until just wilted. Drain through a sieve and leave until cool. Open out 2 large round sheets village bread and fill the inner 15cm (6in) square with the spinach mixture. Top with 3–4 slices fontina cheese, freshly ground black pepper and a squeeze of lemon. Close the bread to form a square. Cook on a griddle or skillet for 5 minutes on the folded side and 3–5 minutes on the other. Quarter to serve.

sausage, caramelized onions and brown sauce

Pick your favourite meaty sausages (or vegetarian, if you prefer) and either bake or slowly fry in a little oil until dark and crunchy (this can take up to 45 minutes). Fry some onions until golden and caramelized – seasoning with salt and freshly ground black pepper (2 large onions will take about 30 minutes). Heat some small thick pitta breads (from Turkish or Lebanese shops). Open up and fill with onions, sausages and brown sauce.

clockwise from top left: melting salmon, crème fraîche and caper; artichoke, rocket and parmesan; sausage, caramelized onions and brown sauce; spinach and fontina cheese

cornbread

Cornbread is both slightly sweet and salty, with a gorgeous nutty taste and texture. It can also be toasted before serving to give it a pleasantly crispy surface. The cornbread keeps for up to 5 days in an airtight container.

175g (6oz/1½ cups) plain
    (all-purpose) flour
1½ tablespoons baking powder
1 teaspoon salt
75g (3oz/½ cup) fine maize
    (cornmeal) or polenta flour
    (this is slightly coarse)
75g (3oz/½ cup) finely ground
    maize (cornmeal) flour
    (this looks like flour)
2 tablespoons sugar
450ml (14fl oz/1¾ cups) milk
3 medium eggs, lightly beaten
75g (3oz/⅓ cup) butter, melted

Coffee choice
filtered black or slightly
    milky coffee made with
    fruity medium roasted
    Kenyan AA beans

Preheat the oven to 200°C, 180–190°C fan-assisted (400°F, gas mark 6). Grease a tin (pan) measuring 18 x 28cm (7 x 11in) and at least 4cm (1½in) deep and line the base with greased greaseproof (waxed) paper.

Sift the flour, baking powder and salt into a large bowl. Stir in the maize (cornmeal) flours and the sugar, then make a well in the centre. Pour the milk, eggs and butter into the centre of the well and mix together, gradually drawing the dry ingredients into the egg mixture. The batter should be quite smooth.

Pour into the prepared tin and bake for 30 minutes until the mixture is well risen, set and the top is golden brown in colour. Allow the cornbread to cool slightly before cutting into 9 rectangles. Serve warm or cold.

   Makes 9

tip
Stale cornbread makes excellent stuffing for turkey, chicken or guinea fowl. Simply rub into crumbs and mix with fried onions, herbs, pine nuts, walnuts or pecans.

morning toast

The modern and conventional way of making toast is, of course, to use a toaster – but this can sometimes be a bit tricky if you like to cut your bread quite thick! Toast made in a toaster tends to be moist and chewy, whereas that made under a grill or in the oven will be crisp, as the bread is dried out more. A griddle or skillet on the hob (stovetop) makes excellent toast, achieving that gorgeous crunchy–chewy texture and the wonderful subtle smokiness that fills the kitchen and really gets your appetite going!

with chocolate

Preheat the oven to 220°C, 200–210°C fan-assisted (425°F, gas mark 7) and preheat a baking sheet. Take two fine textured pieces of white bread with a thick crust. Chop 30–50g (1–2oz/½ cup) plain Valrhona chocolate and sandwich in the centre of the pieces of bread. Toast the sandwich in the oven for 5 minutes, turn and bake for another 3 minutes. Let the sandwich cool, then slice to serve.

Coffee choice caffe latte or cappuccino

with butter and jam

This is probably the simplest form of toast – fresh, flaky crusted French baguette with a soft centre. Spread this 'untoasted toast' with butter and preserves. Choose a butter with character – such as the continental versions, known as lactic butters, which tend to be unsalted or slightly salted. As for the preserves, choose the French high fruit content jams and conserves.

Coffee choice café au lait

with maple butter

This toffee-like butter tastes brilliant on sourdough toast. Bring 300ml (1/2pt/1 1/4 cups) dark maple syrup to the boil in a saucepan. Boil until the syrup reaches 120°C, using a sugar thermometer. Transfer to a bowl and stir in 200g (7oz/7/8 cup) unsalted butter until melted. Whisk with an electric handwhisk for 5–8 minutes until thick and creamy. Store in the refrigerator. Makes 400g (14oz).

Coffee choice **espresso or cappuccino**

with cinnamon

Remove the crusts from 2 pieces thick-sliced white bread, then cut into 2.5cm- (1in-) wide fingers. Beat 2 eggs in a shallow bowl. Mix 3 tablespoons caster (superfine) sugar and 1 teaspoon ground cinnamon on a flat plate. Heat 25g (1oz/2 tablespoons) butter in a pan. Coat the bread with egg, then cook in the pan for 2–3 minutes each side. Drain, then dip in the sugar and cinnamon. Serve with blueberries.

Coffee choice **café au lait or cappuccino**

classics from the bakery

There are certain edibles that are just not worth baking at home, because those available in the shops taste so good. Croissants and brioches are two classic cases. With croissants, choose crisp, flaky ones that don't look too greasy. Brioche should be quite crisp on the outside – not too soft. It makes brilliant toast, too. For a light, textured toast with a subtle vanilla or fruit flavour, opt for the Italian Christmas bread pannetone. Soda breads – plain white, wholemeal or fruit – have a dense cake-like texture and are good for sweet toast.

bolo de arroz

These Portuguese cakes resemble muffins, but are made with rice flour, which gives them a heavy texture. They are excellent served with fresh ricotta cheese and fruits such as galia or charentais melons or strawberries. Arabic, Turkish and Greek grocers all stock the variety of ricotta that is wrapped in paper before being sealed in plastic; tub versions should be reserved for pasta fillings!

Coffee choice café au lait

ricotta with walnut bread

Walnut or hazelnut loaves are almost brown in colour and rather dense in texture with a slightly sweet flavour. They make excellent sweet bruschetta when lightly toasted on a griddle. Brush 1cm- (1/2in-) thick slices of walnut bread with butter and toast on a preheated griddle. Top the warm bruschetta with slices of fresh ricotta cheese, drizzle with dark honey and serve with berries.

Coffee choice espresso

Italian croissant

Heat 350ml (12fl oz/1½ cups) milk, with a split vanilla pod (bean). Remove from heat; cover for 20 minutes. Mix 2 teaspoons cornflour (cornstarch) in 2 tablespoons water; add to 6 tablespoons sugar and 4 egg yolks. Remove pod; add seeds to the egg. Whisk in milk. Cook in a pan for 5–8 minutes; stir until thick. Once cold, stir in 200ml (6½fl oz/¾ cup) double (thick) cream, whipped. Pipe into 8 croissants.

Coffee choice cappuccino or caffe latte

fruit brioche toast

Preheat the oven to 200°C, 180–190°C fan-assisted (400°F, gas mark 6). Cut a 2cm- (¾in-) thick slice of brioche and spread with a thin layer of butter. Slice 2 ripe red-skinned plums and toss in 1 tablespoon warmed clear honey. Put the plums in the centre of the brioche and toast in the oven for 10–12 minutes until the bread is golden and the fruit has softened and started to caramelize.

Coffee choice caffe grande

buffalo mozzarella and proscuitto panini

Panini literally means 'little breads' or rolls. This recipe uses a quick yeast-based Italian flat bread that is cooked in a pan, not in the oven. The recipe makes 10 flat breads – just freeze what you don't need to use immediately. The flat breads only need about 30 minutes to defrost. You can use small ciabatta rolls instead, if you don't feel like making your own bread.

300ml (10fl oz/1¼ cups)
   lukewarm water
½ teaspoon sugar
30g (1¼oz) dried active yeast
1 teaspoon fennel seeds
450g (1lb/4 cups) strong white
   (all-purpose) flour
1 teaspoon salt
1 tablespoon extra virgin
   olive oil

For the filling (for 4 panini)
extra virgin olive oil to drizzle
150g (5oz/1 cup) buffalo
   mozzarella (bocconcini),
   drained and thinly sliced
115g (4oz/2½ cups) roquette
   (arugula)
8–12 wafer-thin slices proscuitto
salt and freshly ground
   black pepper

Coffee choice
caffe grande made with
   dark roasted Tanzanian
   Kilimanjaro beans

Pour about 150ml (5fl oz/⅔ cup) of the water into a small bowl and stir in the sugar. Stir in the yeast, cover and leave in a warm place for the yeast to bubble to double its size (this will take about 5–10 minutes).

Meanwhile, roast the fennel seeds in a dry, hot pan until you can just smell the aromas and the seeds begin to pop. Grind the seeds with a pestle and mortar until quite fine. Mix the fennel seeds with the flour and salt in a large bowl. Make a well in the centre of the dry ingredients and pour in the yeast and oil. Start to mix into the flour, adding the remaining water to form a wet dough.

Turn out the dough onto a lightly floured surface and knead for 10 minutes until the dough is elastic. Place the dough in the bowl, cover with a towel and leave in a warm place for 45 minutes until almost doubled in volume.

Re-knead the dough for 1 minute, then divide into 10 pieces. Using a rolling pin, roll each out to about 1cm (½in) thick and 10cm (4in) diameter; prick all over with a fork.

Heat a heavy-based frying pan or skillet until really hot – it needs to be smoking. Place 2–3 flat breads in the pan. Once the bases are dotted with dark spots, turn the bread over and cook for a further 4 minutes. Stack the rounds of bread and cover with a clean tea towel while cooking the remaining rounds of dough.

For the panini, split 4 breads horizontally with a bread knife. Put cut-side up, on a surface and drizzle with olive oil. Top 4 halves with mozzarella (bocconcini), roquette (arugula) and ruffles of proscuitto. Season with freshly ground black pepper and sandwich with the other halves of flat bread. Toast the panini in a ridged sandwich maker, hot pan or hot oven (about 200°C, 180–190°C fan-assisted [400°F, gas mark 6]) for a matter of minutes until the mozzarella just melts. Halve each panini to serve.

   Makes 10 flat breads; 4 panini

quail's egg and spinach tarts

You can use whatever kind of eggs you like – quail's eggs are good just because of their size, which means 2 eggs per tart. If you choose to use large eggs, just lose a little of the egg white before placing it on the spinach. If you are making these pastries for a special occasion, you can incorporate some fine spears of asparagus – just coat them in olive oil and they will roast up beautifully.

450g (1lb) puff pastry,
   thawed if frozen
1 egg yolk
2 tablespoons milk
25g (1oz/2 tablespoons) butter
450g (1lb) baby spinach leaves
   or pousse
salt and freshly ground
   black pepper
16 quail's eggs
parmesan shavings to serve

Coffee choice
filtered black or milky
   coffee made with medium
   roasted Java beans

Preheat the oven to 220°C, 200–210°C fan-assisted (425°F, gas mark 7).
Roll out the pastry on a lightly floured surface to about 3–5mm (1/8–1/4in) thick. Trim the edges and cut the pastry into 7 x 12cm (2¾ x 4½in) rectangles. Using a thin sharp knife, score a border about 1cm (¾in) all the way around each rectangle, then score with diagonal lines. Prick the centre of each of the rectangles with a fork. Then, transfer the pastries to a baking sheet.

Mix the egg yolk and milk and brush over the pastry rectangles. Chill the pastries for 20 minutes – this prevents the pastry from shrinking on cooking.

Meanwhile, melt the butter in a frying pan and sauté the spinach for about 1–2 minutes until it has just wilted. Drain well through a sieve, squeezing out any excess water by pressing the leaves gently with a wooden spoon. Pat dry on kitchen paper. Season with salt and pepper to taste and set aside until required.

Bake the pastries for 10 minutes until well risen and golden. Carefully push the centres down to form a cavity for the spinach and eggs. Randomly place the spinach in the pastries, leaving 2 wells for the eggs. Add the eggs and season.

Reduce the oven temperature to 190°C, 170–180°C fan-assisted (375°F, gas mark 5) and bake the pastries for a further 12–15 minutes until the base of the pastry is golden and the eggs are just set. Serve warm or cold with shavings of parmesan cheese.

   Makes 8

lemon twists

These are made using a doughnut dough. Fresh doughnuts are delicious – they do take time to make, but everyone will love you for it! If you like, you can roll out the dough, cut out circles and sandwich a blob of jam in the centre. Seal the edges and leave to double in size before deep frying: allow about 2–3 minutes on each side until golden brown. Drain and coat with caster (superfine) sugar while still warm.

200ml (6½fl oz/¾ cup) milk

1 vanilla pod (bean), halved lengthways

115g (4oz/½ cup) caster (superfine) sugar

a pinch of salt

2 tablespoons dried active yeast

300g (11oz/2¾ cups) plain (all-purpose) flour

50g (2oz/¼ cup) butter

3 medium egg yolks

sunflower oil to deep fry

For the lemon glaze

150g (5oz/1¼ cups) icing (confectioner's) sugar

100ml (3½fl oz/5 tablespoons) single (light) cream

2 tablespoons freshly squeezed lemon juice

finely grated lemon rind to decorate

Coffee choice

café au lait made with medium-dark roasted Brazilian Santos beans

Heat the milk with the vanilla pod (bean) to just below boiling point. Pour half of the milk into a small jug and stir in 1 tablespoon sugar and a pinch of salt. Stir in the yeast and leave for 5–10 minutes until it bubbles and doubles in volume. Sift the flour into a large bowl and mix in the remaining sugar. Make a well in the centre, then set aside.

Scrape the seeds out of the vanilla pod and put back into the remaining milk. Discard the pod. Melt the butter and add to the vanilla milk. Pour the vanilla milk and yeast mixture into the centre of the flour, then add the egg yolks. Gradually work the dry ingredients into the liquid until a wet dough is formed. Turn the dough onto a well-floured surface and knead for 5–8 minutes until smooth and elastic. Put the dough in a clean bowl, cover with a tea towel and leave in a warm place for about 1 hour until the dough has risen slightly – it will not double.

While the dough is proving, start the glaze. Put all the ingredients in a heatproof bowl over a pan of simmering water; heat until the sugar dissolves and the mixture is quite warm. Remove the bowl from the pan, cover the surface with clingfilm (plastic wrap), allowing the film to touch the surface directly; this will stop it from forming a crust. Leave until cold. Turn the dough out onto a lightly floured surface and knead for 1 minute. Divide into 12 pieces and keep the rest covered while shaping each piece.

To shape, roll each piece of dough between the palms of your hands and the work surface into a long sausage shape of even thickness, about 1cm (½in) thick. Then bring the two ends together and twist. Press down gently and transfer to a baking sheet. Leave to rest for 15 minutes. (If the dough does not rest, it will untwine on cooking.)

Put the oil in a deep saucepan and heat until 180–190°C (350–375°F), using a sugar thermometer. Fry the twists, in batches of 2–3, for 2 minutes on each side. Drain on kitchen paper. To keep the oil temperature constant, remove the pan from the heat every now and again. If the twists brown too quickly, they will not be cooked through.

Dunk the doughnut twists in the glaze until completely coated. Put on a rack, so that the excess glaze can drip off. Sprinkle with the finely grated lemon rind to serve.

Makes 12

in the afternoon

individual banoffi pies

A restaurant called The Monk, in Sussex, England, came up with the idea of boiling an unopened can of condensed milk for several hours until the milk turned to toffee. This was then poured over sliced bananas in a pastry case and topped with whipped cream. Manufacturers have gone one step further and created ready-to-use jars of banoffi toffee sauce.

115g (4oz/¾ cup) plain
   (bittersweet) Valrhona
   chocolate, melted

For the sweet pastry
225g (8oz/2 cups) plain
   (all-purpose) flour
a pinch of salt
150g (5oz/⅔ cup) chilled
   butter, diced
2 tablespoons caster
   (superfine) sugar
2 large egg yolks
2 tablespoons ice cold water

For the filling
2 bananas
juice of 1 lemon
450g (1lb) jar of banoffi
   toffee sauce or boil a 405g
   (14oz) can of condensed milk
   for 3 hours, then cool
250ml (8fl oz/1 cup) whipping
   (light) cream

Coffee choice
cafetière or filter coffee
   made with mellow-tasting
   medium roasted Jamaican
   Blue Mountain beans

Preheat the oven to 200°C, 180–190°C fan-assisted (400°F, gas mark 6). Make the chocolate curls while making and chilling the pastry cases. Spread the melted chocolate onto a large piece of marble and set aside to cool. If a piece of marble is not handy, turn a large clean baking sheet or tin upside down and spread the chocolate onto this. You may need to chill the chocolate for a few minutes to set. Take a long thin-bladed knife, hold at a 90 degree angle over the chocolate, then gently scrape along the chocolate to create fine curls. Ideally, you should push the knife away from you, but you may find it easier to bring it towards you. Gently lift the curls onto a chilled plate and leave in the refrigerator until required.

For the pastry, mix the flour and salt in a bowl, then rub in the butter to resemble fine breadcrumbs – using a food processor will be faster. In order to control the amount of liquid needed to bind the pastry, return the flour mixture to a bowl, if you are using a food processor, and stir in the sugar. Mix the egg yolks and water in a cup, then stir into the crumb mixture with a fork until large clumps form. Bring the mixture together with your hand to form a dough. Gently knead the dough on a lightly floured surface for 1–2 minutes until smooth. Flatten the dough to a thick disc, cover with greaseproof (waxed) paper and allow to rest in the refrigerator for 20 minutes.

Lightly flour a surface to roll out the pastry thinly – it should be about 3mm (⅛in) thick. Use to line twelve 7.5cm- (3in-) diameter muffin holes in a muffin tray. Prick the bases with a fork and refrigerate for another 20 minutes.

Line the pastry with crumpled greaseproof paper and fill with baking beans (or dry pulses – these become inedible when used for baking blind). Bake the pastries blind for 10 minutes. Remove the beans and paper and cook for another 5 minutes until golden brown. Allow the pastries to cool completely.

Peel and slice the bananas thinly, tossing in the lemon juice to stop them from turning brown. Layer the bananas and banoffi toffee sauce in the pastry cases – at least 2 layers. Whip the cream until soft peaks form, then gently drop a tablespoonful onto each pie. Finish off with a few curls of chocolate to serve.

   Makes 12 pies

mocha-streaked muffins

onion and mustard seed muffins

mocha-streaked muffins

The coffee and the chocolate mixture in this recipe complement each other beautifully, providing the perfect balance of sweet and sharp. The term mocha comes from the Ethiopian port of Mocha, which originally exported the distinctive Mocha coffee bean with its hint of cocoa. For these muffins, use tall dariole moulds. They show off the mocha streaks much more than the conventional small muffin cases.

300g (11oz/2¾ cups) self-raising
  (self-rising) flour
1 teaspoon bicarbonate of soda
  (baking soda)
a pinch of salt
150g (5oz/⅔ cup) golden
  caster (superfine) sugar
2 medium eggs
200ml (6½fl oz/¾ cup) buttermilk

For the mocha
50g (2oz/⅓ cup) plain
  (bittersweet) Valrhona
  chocolate, broken into pieces
75g (3oz/¾ cup) self-raising
  (self-rising) flour
25g (1oz/¼ cup) Valrhona
  cocoa powder
100g (3½oz/scant ½ cup) butter
100g (3½oz/½ cup) dark
  muscavado sugar
1 medium egg, beaten
50ml (1¾fl oz) black coffee
  (half espresso to water), cold

Coffee choice
strong cafetière coffee
  made with medium roasted
  Kenyan AA beans

Preheat the oven to 170°C, 150–160°C fan-assisted (325°F, gas mark 3). Lightly grease the insides of 12 tall dariole moulds with a little butter and line the bases with small circles of greased greaseproof (waxed) paper.

Sift the flour, bicarbonate of soda (baking soda) and salt into a large bowl; stir in the sugar. Make a well in the centre of the dry ingredients and add the eggs and buttermilk. Beat the wet mixture together, then gradually mix in the dry ingredients. The mixture should still be slightly lumpy. Set aside until required.

For the mocha mixture, first melt the chocolate over a pan of simmering water. Sift the self-raising (self-rising) flour and cocoa powder onto a plate. In a bowl, beat the butter and sugar until creamy. Gradually beat in the egg, followed by the cooled melted chocolate and coffee. Fold in the flour and cocoa. Then, gradually fold into the white batter mixture – just enough to streak the mocha mixture through the batter.

Spoon the muffin batter into the prepared moulds, filling them to between halfway and two-thirds full. Bake for 25 minutes until the muffins are well risen and cooked through. Cool slightly before removing from the tins. Serve warm.

  Makes 12

onion and mustard seed muffins

Savoury muffins are perfect food to have on the run or pack and eat later as a snack. There are three important points in the baking of muffins. First, the batter needs to be lumpy, second the muffin cases (large or small) should be filled two-thirds of the way up and third, the baked muffins must be cracked on the top for the perfect appearance.

2 tablespoons olive oil

1 teaspoon black and white (yellow) mustard seeds

3 large Spanish onions, peeled and sliced into fine wedges

knob of butter

salt and freshly ground black pepper

250g (9oz/2¼ cups) plain (all-purpose) flour

2 teaspoons baking powder

½ teaspoon bicarbonate of soda (baking soda)

a pinch of salt

2 tablespoons clear honey

1 large egg, lightly beaten

200ml (6½fl oz/¾ cup) buttermilk

Coffee choice
rich filter or cafetière coffee made with medium roasted Tanzanian Kilimanjaro beans

Preheat the oven to 180°C, 160–170°C fan-assisted (350°F, gas mark 4).

Heat the oil in a large frying pan, then add the mustard seeds and cook for 30 seconds until the seeds start to pop. Quickly stir in the onions, then reduce the heat and allow the onions to cook gently for about 25–30 minutes, stirring every now and again until caramelized. Away from the heat, stir in the butter and season the onions to taste with salt and freshly ground black pepper. Set the onions aside to cool.

Put paper muffin cases in 10 holes of a standard-sized muffin tray. Sift the flour, baking powder, bicarbonate of soda (baking soda) and pinch of salt into a large bowl. Reserve 2 tablespoons of the onions. Stir the remaining onions and honey into the flour mixture, followed by the egg and buttermilk – the batter should still be quite lumpy. Spoon into the prepared cases (only about two-thirds of the way up). Top with the reserved caramelized onions. Bake for 20–25 minutes until the muffins are well risen and golden; a thin knife inserted into a muffin should come out clean. Cool slightly before serving.

Makes 10

ricotta cheesecakes with baked cherries

These are individual lightly baked cheesecakes. The topping is very seasonal, so use fruits such as apricots, peaches or even orange segments when cherries are not around. Using rosemary as a flavouring for fruit is an old Mediterranean tradition, making a modern day comeback – it brings out the sweetness of the fruit in a wonderfully aromatic fashion.

For the base
75g (3oz/6 tablespoons) butter
100g (3¹/₂oz/1 cup) biscuit crumbs,
   finely crushed
finely grated rind of
   ¹/₂ a lemon

For the filling
225g (8oz/1 cup) fresh ricotta
30g (1¹/₄oz/¹/₄ cup) icing
   (confectioner's) sugar
finely grated rind of 1 lemon
juice of ¹/₂ a lemon
1 medium egg
1 medium egg yolk
150ml (5fl oz/²/₃ cup)
   double cream

For the topping
350g (12oz/1²/₃ cups)
   fresh cherries
2 tablespoons clear honey
finely grated rind and
   juice of ¹/₂ an orange
3 sprigs fresh rosemary

Coffee choice
light filter or cafetière coffee
   made with medium roasted
   Mexican Maragogype beans

Preheat the oven to 150°C, 130–140°C fan-assisted (300°F, gas mark 2). Line the 6 holes of a large muffin tray with large paper cases. Melt the butter, transfer to a small jug and leave to stand for 5 minutes to allow the sediment to sink to the base. Put the biscuit crumbs in a large bowl with the lemon rind and pour in the butter, leaving behind the sediment. Stir well and allow to cool slightly. Press the biscuit into the base of the cases, to about 1cm (¹/₂in) thickness. Chill until required.

For the filling, beat the ricotta cheese with the icing (confectioner's) sugar, lemon rind and juice until smooth. Beat in the eggs. Whisk the double cream until soft peaks form, then fold into the ricotta cheese. Spoon this mixture into paper cases, bringing the mixture right to the top and levelling it. Bake for 30 minutes – do not open the oven. Turn off the oven and leave the cakes inside until the oven is completely cold – the cakes will have set to perfection on cooling.

Preheat the oven to 190°C, 170–180°C fan-assisted (375°F, gas mark 5). Wash the cherries and discard the stalks from three-quarters of them. Stone the stalkless cherries. Put all the cherries in a roasting tin (including the unstoned ones) with the honey, orange rind and juice and rosemary sprigs. Roast the cherries for 25 minutes until they are very tender and have begun to caramelize in places. The juices should be quite thick. Leave until completely cold.

Spoon the cherries and the juices over the top of the cheesecakes, ensuring at least 1–2 cherries with stalks are arranged attractively within each pile – add a tiny sprig of rosemary to each cake, if desired. Serve the cheesecakes at room temperature.
   Makes 6

jumbo double chocolate cookies

Intense flavour, richness and chewiness are the three most important criteria for the ultimate chocolate cookie. From this one basic recipe, you can make a couple of changes to create a new cookie (see below). Cookies can be stored in an airtight container for up to 5 days.

225g (8oz/1 cup) unsalted butter,
    softened
225g (8oz/1¼ cups) soft
    light brown sugar
2 large eggs, lightly beaten
1 teaspoon vanilla extract
275g (10oz/2½ cups) plain
    (all-purpose) flour
2 tablespoons Valrhona
    cocoa powder
¾ teaspoon bicarbonate
    of soda (baking soda)
175g (6oz/1¼ cups) plain
    (bittersweet) Valrhona
    chocolate, roughly chopped
butter for greasing

Coffee choice
cappuccino or caffe latte
    made with full-bodied
    dark roasted Tanzanian
    Kilimanjaro beans

Preheat the oven to 180°C, 160–170°C fan-assisted (350°F, gas mark 4). Cream together the butter and the sugar until smooth and fluffy in texture and light in colour – it will be faster using either a food processor or an electric mixer. Then, gradually beat in the eggs and vanilla extract.

Sift the flour, cocoa powder and bicarbonate of soda (baking soda) into a large bowl, then fold into the cookie mixture. Fold in the chocolate pieces, using a plastic spatula to scrape well along the sides of the bowl to ensure that all of the ingredients are mixed together. Chill the mixture for 20 minutes.

Grease 2–3 large baking sheets with butter. You will have to bake in batches as the cookies spread a lot – 3 cookies per baking sheet. Roll the cookie mixture into 15 golf-ball-size balls and place well apart on the baking sheets. Press them down gently with the back of a greased spoon. Bake the cookies for 12–15 minutes until the edges are firm, but the centres are still just soft when gently pressed. Cool for a minute or two before transferring to a wire rack. Serve warm or cold.

Makes 15

other flavour combinations

all-white chocolate
Replace the brown sugar with white caster (superfine) sugar. Melt 100g (3½oz) white chocolate with 100g (3½oz/½ cup) cream cheese and beat into the batter after the eggs are added. Omit the cocoa powder; replace the chocolate pieces with white chocolate.

mocha and hazelnut
Replace 1 tablespoon of the cocoa powder with 1 tablespoon finely ground fresh Mocha coffee beans. Replace the chocolate with 115g (4oz) hazelnut (filbert) shavings.

cream cheese and apricot
Replace brown sugar with white. Beat 200g (7oz/⅞ cup) cream cheese into the batter after adding eggs. Replace cocoa powder with 2 tablespoons ground almonds (almond meal). Use 175g (6oz) chopped no-need-to-soak dried apricots in place of chocolate.

clockwise from top left: all-white chocolate; jumbo double chocolate; cream cheese and apricot; mocha and hazelnut

afternoon toasties

Afternoon toasted sandwiches have a bit more of an edge than morning toast – the breads are richer and may be packed with a strong filling such as spicy chorizo or creamy dolcelatte. The Italians seem to know how to do them best. There are four main groups: the toasted sandwich known as 'toast'; bruschetta – crusty country bread brushed with olive oil, toasted and rubbed with garlic before a topping is added; Pizza Romana – toasted, filled focaccia; and crostini – small slices of a baguette, toasted and topped with an elegant topping.

bruschetta with crispy bacon and avocado

Cut a slice or two from a sourdough bread or ciabatta. (Each slice should be at least 2.5cm [1in] thick.) Brush both sides with olive oil and toast – ideally on a barbecue, but a griddle will do. Rub sliced garlic on the toast. Press down half a peeled ripe avocado onto the bruschetta and season with salt, freshly ground black pepper and a squeeze of lemon juice. Top with grilled bacon or pancetta.

Coffee choice Americano

crostini with goat's cheese and olive paste

Preheat the oven to 200°C, 180–190°C fan-assisted (400°F, gas mark 6). Cut 1.5cm- (1⁄2in-) thick slices from a thin baguette. Brush both sides of each slice with olive oil and toast in the oven for 10 minutes until golden. Spread with black olive paste or tapenade, top with a slice of goat's cheese, sprinkle with capers, drizzle with extra virgin olive oil and grill for 1 minute to heat the cheese. Serve warm.

Coffee choice espresso

Roman-style pizza

Take a piece of focaccia and slice open horizontally. Drizzle both slices with extra virgin olive oil and top one with sliced smoked mozzarella, sliced marinated artichokes, capers and grated parmesan. Put the focaccia sandwich on a very hot skillet. Cook for 4–5 minutes on each side, pressing down with a fish slice. Once the cheese starts to melt, remove and serve immediately.

Coffee choice espresso

Italian toast with provolone and vegetables

Take two slices of white bread and put sliced provolone cheese on one piece. Top with 1–2 tablespoons marinated mushrooms and peppers and season with black pepper. Add some more cheese, then sandwich with the other slice of bread. Toast in a hot ridged sandwich maker for 4–5 minutes (or 3–4 minutes on each side on a preheated griddle) until the cheese melts.

Coffee choice espresso

Madeira loaf cake

Loaf cakes have made a come back – most coffee bars and bakeries now stock a variety. You can change the size of the loaf cake, if you like – this recipe makes a 1kg (2lb) loaf cake, but you can divide the mixture between two 500g (1lb) loaf tins or 8 small individual ones.

175g (6oz/1½ cups) self-raising
   (self-rising) flour
1 teaspoon baking powder
100g (3½oz/1 cup) ground
   almonds (almond meal)
   (see page 72)
175g (6oz/¾ cup) caster
   (superfine) sugar
175g (6oz/¾ cup) unsalted butter,
   softened
3 medium eggs, lightly beaten
finely grated rind and
   juice of 1 orange
25g (1oz/¼ cup) flaked almonds
2 tablespoons apricot jam
   (conserve)
2 tablespoons cold water

Coffee choice
espresso or strong filter coffee
   made with medium-dark
   roasted Kenyan AA beans

Preheat the oven to 170°C, 150–160°C fan-assisted (325°F, gas mark 3). Lightly grease a 1kg (2lb) loaf tin (pan). Line the base with greased greaseproof (waxed) paper. Sift the flour and baking powder into a bowl and stir in the ground almonds. Add the sugar, butter, eggs and orange rind and juice. Beat with a wooden spoon, electric handwhisk or food processor. The mixture should drop easily when lifted with a spoon.

Spoon the cake batter two-thirds up into the tin. Level and sprinkle with flaked almonds. Bake for 1–1¼ hours, covering, if necessary, until well risen and cooked through. (A skewer should come out clean when inserted into the cake.) Cool for 10 minutes, then turn out. Heat the jam and water, pass through a sieve, then brush over the cake.
   Makes a 1kg (2lb) loaf

other flavour combinations

lemon polenta
Replace flour with 75g (3oz/¾ cup) finely ground maize (cornmeal) flour and 75g (3oz/¾ cup) fine maize or polenta flour. Add 1 more teaspoon baking powder. Replace orange rind and juice with grated rind of 3 lemons and juice of 1 lemon. Fold 115g (4oz) blueberries into batter. Omit flaked almonds and glaze. Dust with icing (confectioner's) sugar.

banana with maple syrup
Replace almonds with 1 ripe banana, peeled and mashed. Replace 50g (2oz/¼ cup) of the caster (superfine) sugar with maple syrup and the remaining sugar with soft light brown sugar. Bake as above. Omit flaked almonds and apricot glaze. After baking, cool cake slightly. Boil 100ml (3½fl oz/5 tablespoons) dark maple syrup for 3–5 minutes to 120°C until just caramelized. Remove cake from tin and pour over the syrup. Let cool.

rich chocolate with ganache
Replace 25g (1oz/¼ cup) of the flour with 25g (1oz/¼ cup) Valrhona cocoa powder. Omit the orange rind and juice and replace with 3 tablespoons milk. Fold 75g (3oz) plain (bittersweet) Valrhona chocolate, chopped, into the batter. Omit flaked almonds. Bake as above. Melt 115g (4oz) plain Valrhona chocolate with 75ml (2½fl oz/⅓ cup) double (thick) cream. Away from the heat, beat in 1 tablespoon milk. Cover and set aside until required. Once the cake has cooled, remove from the tin and spread with ganache.

clockwise from top left: banana with maple syrup; rich chocolate with ganache; Madeira; lemon polenta

Portuguese custard tarts

The traditional English custard tarts made with sweet shortcrust pastry and a light custard dusted with nutmeg are delicious. But, for the more adventurous palate, the Portuguese version takes some beating – puff pastry baked at a high temperature, with a deliciously rich vanilla custard. The custard should have large brown caramelized spots for authenticity.

butter for greasing
200g (7oz) ready-rolled puff
   pastry, thawed if frozen
300ml (10fl oz/1¼ cups) double
   (thick) cream
150ml (5fl oz/⅔ cup) milk
1 vanilla pod (bean),
   halved lengthways
50g (2oz/¼ cup) vanilla sugar
6 egg yolks
1–2 tablespoons icing
   (confectioner's) sugar

Coffee choice
stove-top espresso coffee
   made with dark roasted
   Kenyan AA beans

Preheat the oven to 240°C, 220–230°C fan-assisted (up to 500°F, gas mark 9) and preheat a heavy-based baking sheet. Grease 8 holes of a standard muffin tray with butter and line the base with greased greaseproof (waxed) paper. Cut 8 strips from the width end of the pastry, about 1cm (½in) wide. Roll up each pastry strip like a wheel, then roll out with a rolling pin to flatten. Stamp out 5cm- (2in-) diameter circles.

Thinly roll out the remaining pastry to 2mm (⅛in) thickness. Cut out 8 strips about 4cm (1½in) wide and 25cm (10in) long. Use the big strips to loosely line the inside of the prepared muffin tray, placing the prepared circles on the base and pressing them well with your fingers to seal. Chill for 20 minutes, then prick the bases.

Meanwhile, put the cream, milk, vanilla pod (bean) and sugar into a pan and start to heat gently, stirring to dissolve the sugar. Bring to just below boiling point. Remove from the heat. Remove the pod, and scrape the seeds into the milk.

Beat the egg yolks and pour the cream mixture over the top. Strain into a jug. Pour the custard into the pastry cases and dust with icing (confectioner's) sugar. Bake for 25 minutes on the baking sheet until the custard has puffed up and caramelized in places and the pastry is golden brown. Cool for 10 minutes before removing from the tin.

Makes 8

sesame breadsticks

These Cypriot Greek breadsticks are a healthy alternative to biscuits with afternoon coffee. The breadsticks are light, but very crunchy. The sesame seeds need to be boiled in water for 5 minutes, then patted dry on kitchen paper; this way they will stick to the dough more easily and will not burn during baking. The breadsticks can be stored in an airtight container for up to 2 months.

135ml (4½fl oz/7 tablespoons) warm water

1 teaspoon sugar

1 teaspoon active dried yeast

225g (8oz/2 cups) plain (all-purpose) flour

½ teaspoon salt

freshly ground black pepper

1 teaspoon extra virgin olive oil

50g (2oz/⅓ cup) sesame seeds

1 teaspoon fennel seeds

Coffee choice

Turkish coffee or espresso made with dark roasted Yemeni Mocha beans

Pour the water into a small bowl and stir in the sugar and yeast. Leave in a warm place until the yeast is almost doubled in volume. This should take about 5–10 minutes.

Meanwhile, sift the flour and salt into a bowl and stir in plenty of freshly ground black pepper. Add the olive oil and rub into the mixture to form very fine breadcrumbs. Make a well in the centre and add the yeast mixture; gradually draw the dry ingredients into the centre, first with a wooden spoon and then with your hand, to form a wet dough. Turn out the dough and knead on a well-floured surface for 10 minutes until elastic – the dough should spring back when lightly pressed. Return to a clean bowl, cover with a towel and put in a warm place for 1 hour until the dough proves to double its volume.

Meanwhile, put the sesame seeds in a pan and just cover with cold water. Gently bring to the boil and simmer for 5 minutes, drain, pat dry on kitchen paper and spread on a flat tray or large plate. Mix the fennel seeds with the sesame seeds.

Preheat the oven to 180°C, 160–170°C fan-assisted (350°F, gas mark 4). Lightly grease 3–4 baking sheets. Take the dough and divide into 4, then divide one of those pieces into 8. (Keep the dough well under wraps while working.) Take a small piece of dough and roll it into a long sausage shape between your palms and the working surface – roll to about 15cm (6in) long. Put the stick into the tray of sesame and fennel seeds and gently roll over the seeds until coated. Transfer the stick to a prepared baking sheet. Continue with all the dough to make 32 in total.

Bake the breadsticks for 30–35 minutes until lightly golden and hard – they should not be bread-soft. Transfer to cooling racks and leave until cold.

Makes 32 sticks

Italian lemon and pine nut tart

This sweet is a cross between a tart and a pie as the lemon curd filling is enclosed rather than being exposed – it is a lemon tart that you can eat with your fingers! The pastry includes a tiny amount of baking powder to give it a lighter cake-like texture instead of a crisp one.

For the filling

finely grated rind and
  juice of 4 lemons
9 medium eggs
350g (12oz/1½ cups) caster
  (superfine) sugar
250ml (8fl oz/1 cup) double
  (thick) cream

For the pastry

300g (11oz/2¾ cups) plain
  (all-purpose) flour
1 teaspoon baking powder
100g (3½oz/scant ½ cup)
  unsalted butter
115g (4oz/½ cup) caster
  (superfine) sugar
25g (1oz/2 tablespoons)
  vanilla sugar
2 small eggs, beaten
2 tablespoons water
  or vin santo (sweet wine)

To finish

1 large egg yolk
2 tablespoons milk
3 tablespoons pine nuts
icing (confectioner's) sugar
  to dust

Coffee choice

strong cafetière or
  filter coffee made with
  medium-dark roasted
  Sumatra Blue beans

Preheat the oven to 180°C, 160–170°C fan-assisted (350°F, gas mark 4). Start by making the filling. Put all the ingredients in a large heatproof bowl set over a pan of simmering water. Cook for 1 hour, stirring frequently until thick. Remove the bowl from the pan and allow to cool.

For the pastry, sift the flour and baking powder into a bowl. Rub in the butter (use a food processor for speed) until the mixture resembles fine breadcrumbs. Stir in the caster (superfine) sugar and vanilla sugar. Mix the eggs with the water or vin santo, then combine them with the dry ingredients until large clumps form. Bring the mixture together with your hand, to form a dough. Knead gently for 1–2 minutes on a lightly floured surface until smooth. Press to a thick disc, cover with greaseproof (waxed) paper and chill for 30 minutes.

Roll out two-thirds of the pastry and use to line a lightly greased 23cm (9in) fluted, loose-based tart tin (pan) 3.5cm (1⅜in) deep. Spoon in and spread the filling. Roll out the remaining pastry and use to cover the filling, pressing the edges to seal.

Beat the egg yolk with the milk and brush over the pastry top. Sprinkle over the pine nuts. Bake for 40 minutes until well risen and golden brown. Dust with icing (confectioner's) sugar and leave to cool completely for the filling to set. Serve in wedges.
  Serves 8

tip

The filling can be made 2–3 days in advance and stored in the refrigerator or, if you are in a hurry, use ready-made lemon curd (1½, 340g [11oz] jars).

perfect brownies

The credit for this recipe belongs to the food writer Elisabeth Luard. These brownies were cooked for the photo shoot that accompanied a feature of Elisabeth's on chocolate. When the shoot was finished, the photographer telephoned her friends, inviting them to come round for the '...best gooey, chewy chocolate brownies ever...and I can't believe they've been baked by someone over here from England'!

350g (12oz/2⅓ cups) plain (bittersweet) Valrhona chocolate, broken into pieces
250g (9oz/1 generous cup) unsalted butter
50g (2oz/½cup) plain (all-purpose) flour
1 teaspoon baking powder
3 medium eggs, beaten
250g (9oz/1¼ cups) soft brown sugar
175g (6oz/1¾ cups) pecan nuts, roughly chopped

Coffee choice
filter coffee made with medium roasted Costa Rican San Jose beans

Preheat the oven to 170°C, 150–160°C fan-assisted (325°F, gas mark 3). Butter a baking tray measuring 29 x 18.5cm (11½ x 7in) and at least 5cm (2in) deep. Line the base with greased greaseproof (waxed) paper.

Melt the chocolate and butter in a bowl over a pan of simmering water. Once melted, remove from the pan and allow to cool slightly.

Sift the flour and baking powder onto a plate. Whisk the eggs until thick and creamy, then gradually whisk in the sugar. Use an electric mixer fitted with a balloon whisk or an electric handwhisk. The meringue mixture will become really thick and mousse-like and a thick trail will be left on the surface when the beaters are lifted. Gradually fold in the slightly cooled chocolate mixture in stages, alternating with the flour. Fold in the nuts.

Spoon into the prepared tin and bake for 40–45 minutes until the top is cracked and the centre is just firm to the touch. (The brownies should not be of a crumbly consistency like a cake at any time.) Leave to cool in the tin.

Cut the brownies into squares in the tin before turning them out onto a board. Turn the brownies the correct way up. Serve warm or cold.

Makes 15 small squares

tip
Once the brownies are quite cool, you can spread the tops with a generous helping of sweet maple butter spread (see page 37).

after dinner

apricot frangipan tartlets

These delicious apricot tartlets can be made with other fruits too – depending on their availability – figs, cherries or sliced peaches all work beautifully as do soft fruits, such as raspberries and blueberries. Lightly toasting blanched almonds in a hot pan, then grinding them in a food processor, brings out the almond flavour strongly – there is no need to add essence.

1 quantity sweet pastry
   (see page 48)

For the almond frangipan

150g (5oz/1¼ cups) whole
   blanched almonds

115g (4oz/½ cup) unsalted butter,
   softened

75g (3oz/⅓ cup) caster
   (superfine) sugar

2 medium eggs

6 large fresh apricots, halved,
   stoned, then cut into wedges

4 tablespoons apricot jam
   (conserve)

2 tablespoons cold water

Coffee choice

long espresso or Americano
   made with full-bodied dark
   roasted Kenyan AA beans

Preheat the oven to 200°C, 180–190°C fan-assisted (400°F, gas mark 6). Place twelve 6cm- (2½in-) diameter rings onto 2 baking sheets. Divide the pastry into 12 pieces, then thinly roll out each piece to line the metal rings. Trim the top, prick the bases, then chill for 10 minutes. Line each pastry with greaseproof (waxed) paper and fill with baking beans or dried beans. Bake for 10 minutes. Remove the paper with the beans and return the pastries for a further 3 minutes to dry the bases.

For the frangipan, heat a heavy-based frying pan on the hob (stovetop). Add the almonds and toast for 1–2 minutes, so that they begin to release their aroma. Cool the nuts slightly, then whizz them in a food processor until finely ground. In a bowl, whisk the butter and sugar until light and fluffy. Add the almonds; gradually beat in the eggs.

Reduce the oven to 170°C, 150–160°C fan-assisted (325°F, gas mark 3). Spread 3–4 tablespoons frangipan into the base of each tartlet, then stand wedges of fruit in the mixture. Bake the tartlets for 25–30 minutes until the frangipan is just set and the fruit is just starting to caramelize at the tips.

To prepare the glaze, heat the jam with the water, then pass through a sieve. Allow the tartlets to cool for 1 minute, then brush the glaze on the fruit, frangipan and pastry edge. Allow to cool before serving.

   Makes 12

individual plum tartes tatins

These classic French tarts are cooked upside down. Make sure that you turn them out onto their serving plates, so that you catch all of the caramelized juices. Apples are the traditional fruits used for these tarts, but pears or plums are pretty good alternatives.

150g (5oz/generous ½ cup)
   unsalted butter
115g (4oz/½ cup) soft light
   brown sugar
6 large plums, halved and stoned
½ quantity sweet pastry
   (see page 48)

Coffee choice
double or long espresso made
   with full-bodied dark roasted
   Tanzanian Kilimanjaro beans

Preheat the oven to 200°C, 180–190°C fan-assisted (400°F, gas mark 6). Grease a 12-hole patty tray, then line the bases with greased greaseproof (waxed) paper. Beat the butter with the sugar until very creamy. Use about 1 tablespoonful of the butter mixture per patty hole and spread to cover. Then, sit a plum half, cut-side-up, in each of the patty holes.

Roll out the pastry to about 3mm (⅛in) thickness and stamp out 12 circles about 7.5cm (3in) in diameter. Sit each pastry circle on a plum – the pastry needs to be slightly larger than the patty tin, as it will shrink slightly during baking.

Bake the pastries for 15–20 minutes or until golden brown and quite crisp. The juices from the plums and sugar mixture will spill over a little, but that shows that the plums have cooked through and the caramel is forming on the base.

Allow the tarts to stand for 5 minutes before turning them out, as the caramel needs to thicken slightly (this will happen on cooling). Turn out and gently ease away the paper. The tarts are delicious served warm or cold.

Makes 12

chocolate truffles with grappa

white chocolate and cardamom truffles

chocolate truffles with grappa

The quality of chocolate and cocoa powder used for making truffles is crucial – the better the product, the greater the final truffle will taste, so use Valrhona! These truffles are at their best within 3–5 days of making.

575g (1¼lb) plain (bittersweet)
   Valrhona chocolate
450ml (14fl oz/1¾ cups) double
   (thick) cream
2 tablespoons grappa
50g (2oz/½ cup) Valrhona cocoa
   powder

Coffee choice
espresso or caffe freddo
   made with dark roasted
   Tanzanian Kilimanjaro beans

Cut 350g (12oz) of the chocolate into large chunks and put in a bowl. Bring the cream to a rolling boil, then pour over the chocolate and stir, so that the chocolate melts completely. Stir in the alcohol. Now whisk until the mixture is just thick – the whisk should barely leave a trail when lifted.

Leave to cool – this takes at least 4–6 hours but, ideally, leave overnight. On cooling, the mixture will also thicken – now you can make the mixture into balls. Make sure your hands are quite cold – run them under cold water, if necessary (especially your wrists). Take a heaped teaspoonful of mixture and roll it between your hands into a ball about the size of a walnut. Transfer to a tray. Make 30 balls altogether and chill in the refrigerator for about 20 minutes.

Meanwhile, melt the remaining chocolate in a bowl over a pan of simmering water. Allow to cool slightly. Sift the cocoa powder onto a flat plate and place a cooling rack over a large piece of greaseproof (waxed) paper.

Using 2 forks, gently lower a truffle ball into the cooled, yet still runny, melted chocolate. Do not pierce the truffles, just gently manoeuvre them into the chocolate to coat, then scoop out and rest on the rack. Once the chocolate is just set, roll the coated truffles in the cocoa powder.

   Makes 30

other flavour combinations

with ginger
Omit the grappa and add 2 tablespoons finely chopped stem ginger and 2 tablespoons stem ginger syrup just after the chocolate mixture has been whisked.

with mint
Add 6 sprigs fresh mint to the cream while it is being heated. Remove from the cream just before stirring into the chocolate. Omit the grappa.

with chilli
Melt 25g (1oz/2 tablespoons) butter in a frying pan and sauté 1 tablespoon dried chilli flakes. Remove the chillies and add the butter to the cream. Omit the grappa.

white chocolate and cardamom truffles

The blend of cardamom with white chocolate is quite glorious – you really do have to try these truffles! White chocolate is very temperamental, but with the aid of the refrigerator you will not have a problem. The truffles will keep in the refrigerator for 3–5 days.

seeds from 8 cardamom pods
550g (1lb 3oz) white
   Valrhona chocolate
400ml (13fl oz/1²/₃ cups) whipping
   (light) cream
50g (2oz/¼ cup) butter
50g (2oz/½ cup) icing
   (confectioner's) sugar

Coffee choice
espresso or macchiato
   made with dark roasted
   Kenyan AA beans

Crush the cardamom seeds with a pestle and mortar until powdery. Cut 350g (12oz) of the chocolate into small pieces and put into a bowl with the cardamom powder. Heat the cream until just boiling. Stir the cream into the chocolate and cardamom – continue stirring until the mixture is completely smooth. Whisk the chocolate with an electric handwhisk – the mixture will thicken. Allow to thicken until the whisk leaves a trail in the mixture when lifted. Chill for 1–2 hours.

Ensure your hands are quite cold – run your wrists under cold water, if necessary. Take a heaped teaspoon of the mixture and roll it between your palms into a ball about the size of a walnut. The ball should be quite smooth. Place on a tray and repeat to make 34 truffles. Place in the refrigerator for 15 minutes.

Meanwhile, melt the remaining chocolate in a bowl set over a pan of simmering water. Remove the bowl and leave the chocolate to cool, but remain runny. Sift the icing (confectioner's) sugar into a flat dish. Set a cooling rack over greaseproof (waxed) paper.

Take the chilled truffle balls and, using two forks, gently roll each truffle in the chocolate to coat completely, then rest on the cooling rack for the chocolate to set. As soon as the chocolate is set, roll the truffles in the icing sugar to finish them off.
   Makes 34

other flavour combinations

rum and raisin
Soak 115g (4oz/²/₃ cup) raisins, chopped, in 4 tablespoons hot rum for 20 minutes. Omit the cardamom powder and stir the raisins and rum into the warm melted chocolate and cream just after whipping.

rosemary
Omit the cardamom powder and just boil 3–4 sprigs fresh rosemary with the cream. Discard the rosemary and continue as above.

pistachio and saffron
Omit the cardamom powder. Finely grind 100g (3¹/₂oz/1 cup) unsalted pistachios, shelled, and mix into the melted chocolate mixture with a good pinch of saffron.

affogato

This Italian classic, also known as ice cream floats, is one of those desserts that can be put together in minutes, but impresses and satisfies everyone. It is also a great one to have up your sleeve as an alternative dessert if you want to offer two puds at a dinner party. It is traditional to add a shot of alcohol, too – choose from liqueurs such as brandy, amaretto and grappa.

300ml (10fl oz/1¼ cups) milk

300ml (10fl oz/1¼ cups) double (thick) cream

1 vanilla pod (bean)

6 egg yolks

150g (5oz/⅔ cup) caster (superfine) sugar

liqueur of your choice (optional)

Coffee choice

espresso or caffe corretto made with dark roasted Kenyan AA beans to pour onto the ice cream

Ensure the bowl of the ice cream machine is well chilled for the required time in the freezer before you start. (See the manufacturer's instructions.)

Put the milk and cream in a saucepan. Split the vanilla pod (bean) lengthways and add to the pan, then bring the mixture to just below boiling point. Simultaneously, whisk the egg yolks with the sugar. Set the vanilla pod to one side, then pour the warm milk and cream onto the eggs and stir.

Clean the pan and return the custard mixture to the pan, straining it first through a sieve. Return the vanilla pod to the custard mixture and cook over a gentle heat for 5–8 minutes, stirring constantly. At no time should the custard boil – it is thick enough when it coats the back of a large metal spoon. Immediately pour the custard into a large clean bowl so that it does not continue to cook in the pan. Remove the vanilla pod, scrape out the seeds into the custard, then discard the pod. Allow the custard to cool, then chill for at least 30 minutes.

Pour the custard into the ice cream machine and churn for about 10–15 minutes (the time varies between machines). Transfer to a freezerproof container and freeze.

You may wish to remove the ice cream from the freezer about 10 minutes before required, to allow you to make scoops easily. Put single scoops of ice cream into espresso coffee cups and pour over a shot of espresso or caffe corretto coffee. Add a shot of liqueur if desired. Serve immediately with spoons.

Makes 10 ice cream scoops

tip

You don't necessarily have to make your own ice cream – feel free to use one of your favourite ready-made luxury ice creams.

mini chocolate mousse cakes

A gorgeously rich chocolate cake that is a little gooey in the centre. These cakes perfectly finish off a dinner when yes, you really do want a dessert, but just need a taster! You may need two cakes per person for a dinner party serving – it is quite difficult to stop at one!

175g (6oz/1½ cups) self-raising
   (self-rising) flour
1 heaped tablespoon
   Valrhona cocoa powder
115g (4oz/½ cup) unsalted butter
60g (2¼oz/⅓ cup) light or dark
   muscavado sugar
115g (4oz/¾ cup plain
   (bittersweet) Valrhona
   chocolate, broken into pieces
150ml (5fl oz/⅔ cup) black coffee
   (half espresso to water)
1 medium egg
12 raspberries or blackberries
   (depending on the season)
cocoa powder to serve

Coffee choice
mellow-tasting long black
   coffee or Americano made
   with medium roasted
   Jamaican Blue Mountain beans

Preheat the oven to 180°C, 160–170°C fan-assisted (350°F, gas mark 4). Grease 12 small fluted tart tins (pans) – about 5cm (2in) wide and 2.5cm (1in) deep – and line the bases with greased greaseproof (waxed) paper. If you only have 6 tins, work in batches, chilling the mixture in between baking.

Sift the flour and cocoa powder into a bowl and make a well in the centre. Set aside. Put the butter, sugar, chocolate and coffee in a saucepan and heat gently, stirring continuously. All of the ingredients need to melt and gel together to create a thick, runny mixture with a lovely gloss. Pour into the centre of the flour mixture and gradually combine with the dry ingredients. Then, slowly beat in the egg.

Put 2 tablespoons cake mixture in each tin. Bake for 8 minutes – the cakes will still be soft but well risen. Leave to cool and set for 30 minutes – the cakes will dimple in the centre. Remove the cakes from the tins, top each one with a raspberry or blackberry and dust with cocoa powder to serve.

   Makes 12

tip
You could divide the cake mixture between 24 double-thickness petit four cases and bake for 5 minutes. For a large 23cm (9in) round cake, simply bake for 45 minutes until just firm on the top. Remove from the oven and leave at room temperature to cool overnight – it will remain very moussy in the centre. Chilled, the cake becomes firmer and more like a truffle cake. Serve in wedges.

apricot and almond cantucci

There is a whole range of Italian-style fruit and nut biscotti that are ideal after dinner coffee or liqueur accompaniments. These biscotti are rather crunchy, so feel free to do a bit of dunking either in your espresso or vin santo (sweet wine), to soften them up a little. The biscotti can keep fresh for as long as 2–3 months in an airtight container.

250g (9oz/1 generous cup) caster (superfine) sugar

2 large eggs

1 teaspoon orange blossom water

250g (9oz/2¼ cups) Italian tippo 00 flour

1 teaspoon bicarbonate of soda (baking soda)

a pinch of salt

115g (4oz/¾ cup) unpeeled (raw) almonds

115g (4oz/½ cup) dried apricots, roughly chopped

1 egg yolk with 2 tablespoons milk to glaze

caster (superfine) sugar to sprinkle

butter for greasing

Coffee choice
espresso, caffe freddo
  or caffe corretto
  made with dark roasted
  Brazilian Santos beans

Preheat the oven to 150°C, 130–140°C fan-assisted (300°F, gas mark 2). Line two baking sheets with greased greaseproof (waxed) paper. Whisk the sugar, eggs and orange blossom water using an electric handwhisk until a thick creamy mousse is formed (about 4–5 minutes). Sift the flour, bicarbonate of soda (baking soda) and salt into the mixture and fold in. Mix in the almonds and apricots to form a sticky dough.

Turn out the mixture onto a well-floured surface and shape into 3 sausage shapes about 7.5cm (3in) wide and 12.5cm (5in) long. Place onto the baking sheets, spaced well apart, brush the surface with the glaze and sprinkle with sugar. Bake the biscotti for 30–35 minutes until slightly risen and golden brown. Remove from the oven and set aside until cool enough to handle. If too cold, the almonds will not cut well.

Reduce the oven to 130°C, 120°C fan-assisted (250°F, gas mark 1). Gently slide the biscotti onto a cutting board and cut with a bread knife into thin slices, 5mm (¼in) thick. Return to the baking sheets, resting each biscotti on its side. Bake for 20–25 minutes, turning over halfway through cooking. Cool before serving.

Makes 40

other flavour combinations

chocolate and pistachio
Omit the orange blossom water and apricots. Replace the almonds with pistachios and add 175g (6oz) plain (bittersweet) Valrhona chocolate, chopped.

polenta and aniseed
Omit the almonds, apricots and orange blossom water. Before adding the flour to the batter, add 4 tablespoons fine maize (cornmeal) or polenta flour, plus 2 tablespoons pernod, the finely grated rind of 1 lemon and 1 tablespoon aniseed seeds.

prune and brandy
Replace 50g (2oz/¼ cup) of the caster (superfine) sugar with vanilla sugar. Soak 175g (6oz) ready-to-use pitted prunes in 4 tablespoons brandy. Drain the prunes, reserving the juice, and chop them into pieces. Replace the almonds, apricots and orange blossom water with the prunes and 1½ tablespoons prune juice.

clockwise from top left: polenta and aniseed; chocolate and pistachio; apricot and almond; prune and brandy

brown sugar and hazelnut meringues

The use of brown sugar gives these meringues a vanilla-like flavour. The general rule is double sugar to egg whites. How you measure your egg whites is up to you – weigh the egg whites, so that you know exactly how much sugar to use. Another great tip is to warm the egg whites and sugar a little before you use them – this also helps towards achieving perfect meringues!

150g (5oz) egg whites

300g (11oz/1¾cups) soft light
   or dark brown sugar

40g (1½oz/⅓cup) hazelnuts
   (filberts)

Coffee choice
espresso or espresso corretto
   made with full-bodied dark
   roasted Kenyan AA beans

Preheat the oven to 150°C, 130–140°C fan-assisted (300°F, gas mark 2).
Put the egg whites and sugar in a bowl set over a pan of simmering water, stirring occasionally until the sugar dissolves. The mixture will become quite warm. Meanwhile, make shavings from the hazelnuts (filberts), using a small truffle shaver or vegetable peeler. Alternatively, use a coarse grater or just chop thinly.

Remove the bowl from the pan and whisk the egg white mixture with an electric mixer for about 15 minutes – the mixture will stiffen on cooling. Fold in three quarters of the hazelnuts. Line 3 baking sheets with baking parchment or non-stick silicon paper. Spoon the meringue onto the baking sheets – about 2 teaspoons per meringue – spacing them well apart. Use the back of a small spoon to make swirls on the meringue to give it that rustic look. Sprinkle with the remaining hazelnuts.

Bake the meringues for 15 minutes, then turn off the oven – but do not open the door. Leave in the oven overnight – this way the meringues will not brown; some of the sugar will seep out and caramelize. Serve cold.
   Makes 18

tip
Brown sugar meringues topped with crème fraîche and coffee granita (see page 21) are delicious. Make some caramel (see page 88) and drizzle around a small mound in the centre of the plate. Finish off with segments of orange.

caramel

DRY METHOD Place the sugar in a pan and heat until it dissolves to a liquid and turns amber. It is important to swivel the sugar constantly. This method is very fast and requires your fullest attention – it is not suitable for electric hobs (stovetops).

WET METHOD Put the sugar in a pan with water – 150ml (5fl oz/$^2/_3$ cup) to every 450g (1lb/2 cups) sugar – heat gently until the sugar dissolves, stirring occasionally. Now boil the sugar while swivelling the pan (not stirring) to achieve the desired colour of caramel.

iced crystal balls

Make small melon ball scoops of ice cream of your choice – vanilla, chocolate, toffee or almond. Place the scoops on a well-chilled baking sheet and return to the freezer. Make the caramel using 450g (1lb/2 cups) sugar. Pour the caramel onto a greased baking sheet and leave until cold. Then, crush the caramel into fine crystals and use it to coat the ice cream balls.

Coffee choice espresso

hokey pokey

Line the base and sides of a small square tin with well-oiled baking parchment. Use 450g (1lb/2 cups) sugar to make the caramel. Away from the heat, whisk in 2 teaspoons bicarbonate of soda (baking soda) for about half a minute and pour into the tin. Leave to cool. Remove from the tin and break into chunks. You could coat half of each piece with melted chocolate.

Coffee choice espresso macchiato

nut brittle

Use a non-stick baking sheet or silicon sheet. Gently toast 300g (11oz/2¾ cups) whole blanched almonds, skinned hazelnuts (filberts), pistachios or 75g (3oz) sesame seeds. Use 450g (1lb/ 2 cups) granulated sugar to make the caramel. Stir the nuts or sesame seeds in the caramel and pour onto the prepared baking sheet. Leave to cool, then break into shards to serve.

Coffee choice espresso or caffe corretto

toffee lychees

These are rather dramatic-looking. Peel the lychees and pat them dry. Suspend a cake rack over a large deep bowl. Make the caramel using 450g (1lb/2 cups) sugar. Dip the lychees in the caramel, then place on the rack, allowing the caramel to form long strands. Leave to set. (Alternatively, you could use figs, apricots or cherries for this recipe – wipe them clean before use.)

Coffee choice espresso

galatobourekia

Traditionally, these Greek custard-filled phyllo pastries are sold in large rectangles steeped in syrup. You can serve them with afternoon Turkish coffee or with after dinner coffee. These pastries can be prepared in advance, and frozen before baking (as long as the pastry was fresh and not frozen). Cook the pastries from frozen for 40 minutes.

For the custard
300ml (10fl oz/1¼ cups) milk
50g (2oz/½ cup) fine semolina
5 tablespoons caster
   (superfine) sugar
1 teaspoon orange blossom water
1 egg yolk

For the syrup
250g (9oz/1 generous cup)
   granulated sugar
150ml (5fl oz/⅔ cup) water
2 strips thinly pared lemon rind

For the pastries
200g (7oz) phyllo pastry
3 tablespoons sunflower
   or vegetable oil

Coffee choice
Turkish coffee made
   with dark roasted
   Yemeni Mocha beans

Ideally, make the custard the day before and leave to set solid. Mix all the custard ingredients in a heavy-based saucepan and gently heat, stirring constantly. Do not boil, but cook until the custard is very thick. Pour the custard into a shallow dish and leave until cold. Chill in the refrigerator overnight, if possible.

Make the syrup before you start to make the pastries, as it needs to be completely cold when added or the pastries will become soggy. Put all of the syrup ingredients into a heavy-based saucepan and heat gently until the sugar dissolves. Bring to the boil and cook for 5 minutes until a thick syrup forms – it should not turn amber at any time. Allow to cool, discarding the lemon rind after at least 30 minutes of cooling.

   Preheat the oven to 180°C, 160–170°C fan-assisted (350°F, gas mark 4).
Cut the phyllo pastry into twenty-five 18 x 15cm (7 x 6in) oblong strips. Place a heaped teaspoon of custard at one end of a strip, roll the pastry a third of the way, then bring the sides over to completely enclose the custard, before continuing to roll up. Each galatoboureko should be about 10cm (4in) long and 1.5cm (½in) thick. Don't be tempted to put too much filling in each pastry or they will explode during cooking!

Bake all of the galatobourekia in a large roasting tin drizzled with the oil for 20 minutes until they are golden in colour and crisp. Drain off any excess oil from the roasting tin, pour in the cold syrup and swirl the tin around to coat the pastries completely. Drain and leave to cool. Serve cold.
   Makes 25

pistachio cookies

These meringue-based nutty cookies are light in texture with an almost melt-in-the-mouth effect and a subtle crispy bite. Just like meringues, these cookies freeze well for up to 2 months in an airtight container.

150g (5oz/1 cup) shelled
  unsalted pistachios
175g (6oz/3/4 cup) caster
  (superfine) sugar
3 tablespoons finely grated
  orange rind
50g (2oz/1/2 cup) plain
  (all-purpose) flour
3 large egg whites
2 tablespoons icing
  (confectioner's) sugar

Coffee choice
granita or caffe corretto
  made with dark roasted
  Brazilian Santos beans

Preheat the oven to 180°C, 160–170°C fan assisted (350°F, gas mark 4). Line 2 baking sheets with greased parchment paper. Put three-quarters of the pistachios in a food processor and finely grind (don't worry if the odd piece remains quite large). Transfer the pistachios to a bowl and stir in 115g (4oz/1/2cup) of the caster (superfine) sugar and all the orange rind, then sift in the flour.

In a separate bowl, whisk the egg whites until soft peaks form. Gradually whisk in the remaining caster sugar – the mixture should become glossy and stiff. Fold the egg whites into the pistachio mixture with a plastic spatula.

Place heaped teaspoons of the cookie mixture, in oval shapes, onto the prepared baking sheets, making sure that you space them well apart. Shave the remaining pistachios over the cookies using either a small truffle shaver or vegetable peeler or just chop thinly. Bake for 12 minutes until quite puffy, just browned and set on the base. Dust with icing (confectioner's) sugar and leave to cool for 10 minutes before removing with a palette knife onto a cake rack to cool. Serve cold.

Makes 30

index

Abyssinia 10
affogato 81
Americano 20, 58, 72, 82
apricot frangipan tartlets 72
arabica 10, 13
    AA 10
    caffeine content 10
    Estate 10
    Supreme 10
aroma 10, 14

banoffi pies, individual 48
bean(s)
    arabica 10, 13
    groups 10
    robusta 10, 13
biscotti 85
blending 14
blends 10, 14
bolo de arroz 38
Brazil/ Brazilian 10
    Bourbon Santos 13
    Santos beans 13, 45, 85, 93
breadsticks, sesame 64
breakfast muffins 30
brewing methods 19
brioche 38, 39
brownies, perfect 68
bruschetta 58

café au lait 23, 36, 37, 38, 45
cafe con leche 23
cafetière(s) 13, 17
    coffee 48, 52, 53, 54, 67
    method 19
caffe
    corretto 21, 81, 85, 86, 89, 93
    freddo 21, 78, 85
    grande 20, 26, 32, 39, 41
    latte 23, 30 36, 39, 57
    latte freddo 20
caffeine content 14
    arabica 10
cappuccino 22, 23, 24, 30, 36, 37,
    39, 57
caramel 86, 88, 89
Central Africa 10
Central America 10
cheesecakes, ricotta with baked
    cherries 54

chocolate
    cookies 57
    with ganache loaf cake 60
    mocha-streaked muffins 52
    mousse cakes, mini 82
    brownies 68
    and pistachio cantucci 85
    truffles 78, 79
coffee granita 21, 86, 93
coffee oils 10, 14
Colombia/Colombian 10
    San Augustin 13
Congo 10
Continental roast 14
cookies 57, 93
cornbread 35
Costa Rican San Jose 13, 68
crema 10, 20, 21
croissant(s) 38, 39
croque monsieur 26
crostini 58
custard tarts, Portuguese 63

dark roast 14
decaffeination 14

elephant bean 13
espresso 10, 14, 20, 37, 38, 58, 59,
    60, 63, 64, 70, 72, 78, 79, 81,
    85, 86, 88, 89
    macchiato 21, 79, 88
    machines 17, 19
    method 19, 20
    variations 20, 21
Ethiopia/Ethiopian 10, 13
    Mocha 13, 31

filter coffee 13, 17, 31, 35, 42, 46,
    48, 53, 54, 60, 67, 68
    machines 17
    method 19
flat breads 32
    see also panini
galatobourekia 90
grinding 17

Harar Longberry 13
hokey pokey 88

ibrik 17, 19

ice cream
    affogato 81
    iced crystal balls 88
India/Indian 13
Indonesia/Indonesian 13

Jamaica/Jamaican 10
    Blue Mountain 13, 48, 82
Java 13
    beans 42
jug method 17, 19

Kenya/Kenyan 10
    AA 13, 30, 35, 52, 60, 63, 72,
        79, 81, 86
    Estate 13
    Peaberry 13, 32

lemon
    and pine nut tart, Italian 67
    twists 42
loaf cakes
    banana with maple syrup 60
    lemon polenta 60
    Madeira 60
    rich chocolate with ganache 60
long espresso 20, 63, 72, 75
lychees, toffee 89

Madeira loaf cake 60
meringues
    brown sugar and hazelnut 86
    pistachio cookies 93
Mexican Maragogype 13, 54
Mexico/Mexican 10
milky coffee 23, 35, 42
mocha
    and hazelnut cookies 57
    -streaked muffins 52
Monsooned Malabar Mysore 13
muffins 30–31, 52–53

nut brittle 89

onion and mustard seed
    muffins 53

pain au chocolat 38
panini, buffalo mozzarella and
    proscuitto 41

percolator(s) 8, 17, 19
pies, individual banoffi 48
pistachio
    cookies 93
    and saffron truffles 79
Pizza Romana 58
plum tartes tatin, individual 75
pulverized coffee 17, 19

quail's egg and spinach tarts 42

raspberry streusal muffins 31
ricotta
    with bolo de arroz 38
    cheesecakes with baked
        cherries 54
    with walnut bread 38
Ristretto 20
roasting 14
robusta 10, 13
Romano 20
Roman-style pizza 59

salmon, crème fraîche and caper
    flat bread 32
sandwiches 26, 32, 36, 41, 59
Santos beans 13
sesame breadsticks 64
South America/South American 10
South East Asia 10
Sumatra Blue 13, 67
sweet pastry 48, 67

Tanzanian Kilimanjaro 13, 26, 41,
    53, 57, 75, 78
tart(s)
    individual plum tartes tatin 75
    Italian lemon and pine nut 67
    Portuguese custard 63
    quail's egg and spinach 42
toast 26, 36, 37, 39, 59
truffles 78, 79
Turkish coffee 13, 17, 19, 64, 90

walnut bread, ricotta with 38
West Africa 10
white chocolate and cardamom
    truffles 79

Yemeni Mocha beans 13, 64, 90

directory

roasting shops – UK

Algerian Coffee Stores Ltd,
52 Old Compton Street,
London W1V 6PB;
tel: 020 7437 2480;
fax: 020 7437 5470
www.algcoffee.co.uk

Brian Wogan Ltd,
2 Clement Street, Bristol BS2 9EQ;
tel: 0117 955 3564;
fax: 0117 954 1605
www.wogan-coffee.co.uk

Camden Coffee Shop,
11 Delancy Street, London NW1;
tel: 020 7387 4080

Godfrey Williams and Sons;
9 and 11 The Square, Sandbach,
Cheshire CW11 1AP;
tel: 01270 762 817

HR Higgins Ltd,
79 Duke Street, London W1K 5AS;
tel: 020 7629 3913;
fax: 020 7499 5912
www.hrhiggins.co.uk

Kafe Da,
18 Bedford Street, Norwich NR2 1AJ;
tel: 01603 622 836

Keith's Tea and Coffee
Specialist Store, 2 Blackjack Street,
Cirencester GL7 2AA;
tel: 01285 654 717
(Mail order on: irvings@lineone.net)
www.keiths.co.uk

Markus Coffee Co Ltd,
13 Connaught Street,
London W2 2AY;
tel: 020 7723 4020

The Roast and Post Coffee Co,
84 High Street, Tonbridge TN9 1AP;
tel: 01732 770 657;
fax: 01732 770 315
www.Realcoffee.uk

The Tea and Coffee Plant,
170 Portobello Road,
London W11 2EB;
tel: 020 7221 8137
www.coffee.uk.com

Wilkinson's Coffee
and Tea Merchants,
5 Lobster Lane,
Norwich NR2 1DQ;
tel: 01603 625 121
(Plus mail order service.)

ingredients – UK

Chandos Deli,
121 Whiteladies Road,
Bristol BS6 6LJ;
tel: 0117 970 6565

Coopers Food Hall,
65–67 Bold Street, Liverpool L1 4EZ;
tel: 0151 707 8251

Mackintosh of Marlborough,
42a High Street, Marlborough,
Wiltshire SN8 1HQ;
tel: 01672 514 069

Porcini,
The Laurels, Tubbs Lane,
Highclere, Newbury,
Berks RG20 9RD;
tel: 01635 250 847
www.porcini.co.uk

Turkish Food Centre,
89 Ridley Road,
London E8 2NP;
tel: 020 7254 6754

Valvona & Crolla Ltd,
19 Elm Row,
Edinburgh EH7 4AA;
tel: 0131 556 6066;
fax: 0131 556 1668

Villandry,
170 Great Portland Street,
London W1W 5QB;
tel: 0207 631 3131

equipment – UK

Gaggia,
Homeware Brands Ltd,
Crown House, Mile Cross Road,
Halifax, West Yorkshire HX1 4HN;
tel: 01422 330 295;
fax: 01422 330 414
www.homewares.co.uk

Margaret Howell,
29 Beauchamp Place,
London SW3 1BR;
tel: 020 7584 2462;
fax: 020 7584 6925

Mint,
70 Wigmore Street,
London W1U 2SF;
tel: 020 7224 4406;
fax: 020 7224 4407

Nicole Farhi Home,
17 Clifford Street,
London W1X 6SL;
tel: 020 7494 9051;
fax: 020 7494 9052

Selfridges, London
400 Oxford Street,
London W1A 1AB;
tel: 020 7629 1234;
fax: 020 7495 8321

Selfridges, Manchester
1 The Dome, The Trafford Centre,
Manchester, M17 8DA;
tel: 0161 629 1234;
fax: 0161 629 1111

Summerill and Bishop Ltd,
100 Portland Road,
London W11 4LN;
tel: 020 7221 4566;
fax: 020 7727 1322

Vessel,
114 Kensington Park Road,
London W11 2PW;
tel: 020 7727 8001;
fax: 020 7727 8661

roasting shops – Australia

Belaroma Trading,
457 Penshurst Street,
Roseville,
NSW 2069;
tel: 61 2 9417 5193
(Good for ingredients.)

Cafe Hernandez,
60 King's Cross Road,
Potts Point,
NSW 2011;
tel: 61 2 9331 2343

The Coffee Roaster,
117 Arundel Street,
Glebe,
NSW 2037;
tel: 61 2 9552 6279

Grinders Coffee House,
277 Lygon Street,
Carlton,
VIC 3053;
tel: (03) 9416 4169

roasting shops – USA

Boulevard Coffee
Roasting Company,
590 Fair Oaks Boulevard,
Carmichael,
California 95608 USA;
tel: 1 916 973 0640
boulevardcoffee.com

The Fresh Bean Coffee Company,
1205 Washington Drive,
Stafford,
Virginia 22554 USA;
tel: 1 540 657 0123;
fax: 1 540 657 9426
www.freshcoffee.com

Longo Coffee & Tea Inc,
201 Bleeker Street,
New York,
NY 10012 USA;
tel: 1 212 477 5421;
fax: 1 212 979 2303
www.portorico.com